ESSENTIAL READING SKILLS OF JOURNEYS GRADE 1 UNIT 1A

for

SMARTIES

A Teacher Presentation Manual
To Simplify the Delivery of
The Basic Reading Skills,
Volume 1
Lessons: Kindergarten Transition - 2

Bruce Farr, Ed.D.

Table of Contents

INTRODUCTION –
USING *ESSENTIALS*

Last Summer, while on vacation, I was invited to attend a first grade class. The teacher explained that she was teaching reading with the *Houghton Mifflin Journeys* first grade program. She knew I was a retired first grade teacher. She invited me to observe the teaching of reading.

After the session we discussed the reading program. I suggested that it would be helpful if the phonic skills and vocabulary were pulled together and made into a presentation manual. She was enthusiastic about the possibility. "It would streamline my teaching,"

This presentation manual is the result of that experience. It draws upon my teaching experience and parallels the basic reading content in *Houghton Mifflin Journeys Grade 1*. This first unit is divided into two manuals around two hundred pages. They will facilitate Direct Instruction.

One thing I know, you have to be smart to teach first graders. They keep you busy all day long!

I trust that *Essentials* will save you time and streamline the teaching of *Houghton Mifflin Journeys Grade 1*.

ABOUT THIS BOOK:

Essentials of Journeys Grade 1 is a supplement to *Houghton Mifflin Journeys Grade 1 Unit 1*. *Essentials* filters out the essential word attack skills of *Houghton Mifflin Journeys Grade 1 Unit 1* and gathers them for the teacher to access in a daily approach to reading.

The content of this book (*Essentials of Journeys Grade 1 Unit 1A*) parallels the skills in the lessons in *Houghton Mifflin Journeys Grade 1 Unit 1*.

Essentials only focuses on word attack skills which will form the basis for all reading skills that follow. *Essentials* will allow the teacher to concentrate during a focused period on word attack skills and vocabulary recognition. *Essentials* is just one of the tools in the teacher's tool box to help teach reading.

The decodable readers in *Houghton Mifflin Journeys Grade 1 Unit 1* are similar in vocabulary to the lessons in *Essentials*.

THE ESSENTIAL SKILLS OF READING

1- LEFT TO RIGHT EYE TRAINING

Students must train their eyes to see a word from left to right. This is accomplished in *Essentials* by providing left to right training with every word. Prompts under the words gives the teacher the opportunity to move his/her finger from left to right under the word. This trains the students to see words in a left to right sequence. To illustrate this left to right focus, you must compare the difference between the words "how" and "who." If it was not for the sequence of the letters in these words, they would be indistinguishable. The sequence makes the difference in the eventual sight recognition of words.

2- PHONEMIC WORD ATTACK SKILLS

In beginning reading, the students need to have skills to attack words, a way to discover the word for themselves. Phonemic skills afford the quickest way to provide independence in discovering words. Starting with a few sound recognition skills and building a basic vocabulary does that. *Essentials* provides a consistent strategy to teach the sounds and then immediately use them in attacking words. It pulls the vocabulary in the lesson together in one place and gives the teacher the opportunity to provide meaningful repetitions with the students to commit the vocabulary to memory.

3- HIGH FREQUENCY WORD STRATEGIES

Journeys Grade 1 Unit 1 requires an abundance of high frequency words to allow meaning to the Anchored Text. *Essentials* gives the teacher the ability to use sight word strategies to teach these words to the students. See "HIGH FREQUENDCY WORD STRATEGIES" below.

4- READING STORIES THAT USE THE TAUGHT VOCABULARY

Essentials provides simple stories to read that exclusively use the vocabulary that has been taught in the day's lesson. This gives success to students. The student is never faced with words that he/she has not already attacked with the teacher's instruction. The student has the skills to attack each word. This gives the teacher an ability to maintain an assessment of the student's skills. If the student is unable to attack the words, then the student needs more help in the immediate lesson until he/she is able to successfully read the vocabulary of the story.

Studies have shown that a student cannot get comprehension from a passage unless he/she recognizes 80% of the vocabulary. *Essentials* provides the stories that have 100% capabilities to recognize the vocabulary. An evaluation of the words that a student misreads will lead to the development of an instructional plan that will correct the errors.

5- REPITITION & PRACTICE

Essentials is designed to keep reviewing the vocabulary, both phonetic and sight, to maintain the recognition of the words in the students' memories. The sounds, sounding it out practice, sight word practice, and story vocabulary continually repeat for maximum practice. The formats allow the teacher to repeat and check student understanding by repetition.

IMPORTANT TEACHING SKILLS

1-SOUNDING OUT WORDS FOR STUDENTS TO HEAR AND REPEAT:

WHEN SOUNDING A WORD OUT DO NOT STOP BETWEEN THE SOUNDS. The sounding out formats begin each daily lesson. The words are printed with phonetic spelling and appropriate letter timing. Some letters are quick sounds while others are sustained sounds. Here is an example:

$$\text{sssss} - \text{aaaaa} \text{ -t}$$
$$* \qquad * \qquad >$$
(Sustained   Sustained   Quick)

When the students hear sounds together they can say the word. Separating sounds does not lend to easy recognition.

2-USE OF SIGNALS

Essentials encourages the use of signals. Giving a group signals allows the teacher to evaluate the responses of the students. She/he can hear and see wrong responses and can immediately make corrections.

Prompts are placed under word practice formats to show finger placement when practicing the word. The prompts are the following:

@ - **Start with your finger here**
* - **Sustained sound (hold for 1-2 seconds)**
> - **quick sound (move quickly to the next sound)**
^ - **Spell it out / say the name of the letter**
** - **This indicates that the "s" is sounded as a "z."**
>> - **continue moving your finger in this direction**
x-**Do not sound this letter.**
?-**Sounds wrong/Guess the word by content or "what sounds right?"**

PHONETIC WORDS: The students sound the word out as the teacher loops the finger from left to right from sound to sound.

HIGH FREQUENCY / SIGHT WORDS: In the sight word format the teacher (1) tells the students the word, (2) has the students repeat the word, (3) has the students spell the word as the teacher points to each letter, and (4) has the students repeat the word again.

3- STORY PROMPTS FOR STURGGLING READERS:

The sound/letter prompts are provided for the stories to enable the teacher to sound out or spell out words with the struggling reader. The struggling reader may become overwhelmed by the words in the story until he/she is able to see and practice them as words. It is suggested for the struggling reader the following strategy for reading the story:

a. Read the story one word at a time, sounding/spelling each word and repeating it.
b. Read the story one word/one sentence at a time without sounding out the words.
c. Reread each sentence.
d. Read the story one sentence at a time.
e. Read the story as a whole.

4-HIGH FREQUENCY WORD STRATEGIES

High frequency words are also called high utility words. These words in *Houghton Mifflin Journeys Grade 1 Unit 1* are introduced to help the student obtain more meaning from the Anchored Texts found in each lesson. Either (1) these words are at a difficulty level that keeps the students from "sounding them out" (the student does not know all the sounds) or (2) the words cannot be "sounded out" because they do not follow phonetic rules.

(1) Some of the high frequency words can later be "sounded out." Such a word is introduced in the first week for the story *What is a Pal.* The students can sound out the word "pal" in lesson three, after the teacher introduces the "l" sound. The student cannot sound "pal" out in lesson one where the word it introduced. Therefore it becomes a "high frequency" word.

(2) Other words the student cannot "sound out" because they do not follow the rules of phonics. When a student memorizes words, the words are referred to as "sight words."

The three ways to learn "sight words" are the following:

1- Say the word, spell the word, then repeat the word again. Repetition will help to memorize the word.

2- Sounding the word out wrong then saying the word right is the mnemonic approach to memorizing words. The student can only do this if he/she knows all the sounds in the word. Typical example is the word "was." We sound it out wwwww-aaaaa-sssss but say "wuz." This approach clues the student to the word by associating the pronunciation of the sounds in the word with the correct saying of the word.

3- Sometimes we can be creative with the word and associate the word with something that will evoke the correct response. An example is associating the word "I" with the name of the letter or drawing eyes in the two "o's" in the word "look." This approach takes teacher creativity.

Essentials of Journeys Grade 1 attempts to use all three of these methods.

5-ASSESSMENT THROUGH USE OF FOLLOW UP ACTIVITIES:

There are stories for each day's lesson. These stories are designed with vocabulary that the student should master. They should have mastery of the sounds for the words that are phonetic and memorization of the high frequency words. Both phonetic words and high frequency words are in the stories.

The teacher can conclude each lesson listening to an oral reading of the daily story with each child. This is a daily assessment of the reading ability of each child. Each student can be successful at reading the story if they have mastery of the words. If a student is unsuccessful, then the student has not learned the skills up to that lesson. The errors or lack of mastery should immediately be remediated with that particular student. The teacher can diagnose the problem and provide the instruction and practice to insure success. The teacher may choose group instruction or individual instruction.

The "Take-It-Home" is a repeat of the story in the lesson. Students can return to their seats and read to themselves or to each other. They also have space on the "Take-It-Home" to draw a picture of the story based upon their comprehension. Later, the teacher can ask the student about the picture to determine the student's comprehension.

Each lesson has a corresponding 'handprinting' exercise. This gives the student the opportunity to practice printing and to experience some of the words in the story. It gives the teacher time to work with other students.

At the end of the day the Take-It-Home can go home with the student. Teachers can use this opportunity to encourage parents to read with their child. The parent can assess their student's success by listening to their child read.

The following pages are a sample of the Take-It-Homes.

Name: _____

Date: _____

Parents: Your child is successful in reading in the classroom if he or she can read this without mistakes. Take time to read the Take-It-Home with your child every day. If you do, you are helping your child learn to read. ***The Italicized words are words that your child needs to memorize.*** The other words your child can "sound out."

Dan *has*z *a* bat.
He can hit *a* big bag.
*His*z pig bit *the* bag.

Name: _____ Date: _____

Dan has a bat and bag.

His pig bit the bag.

x

KINDERGARTEN TRANSITION DAY 1:

HEARING SOUNDS IN WORDS: (Phonemic Awareness)
Model these words slowly. Students respond upon your signal, "What word?"

**DO NOT STOP BETWEEN THE SOUNDS...
==

aaaaa-mmmmm .... (**am**)		d-aaaaa-d .... (**dad**)
mmmmm-aaaaa-nnnnn .... (**man**)		mmmmm-ooooo-p .... (**mop**)
aaaaa-t .... (**at**)		fffff-aaaaa-nnnnn .... (**fan**)
k-aaaaa-t .... (**cat**)		mmmmm-aaaaa-p .... (**map**)
sssss-aaaaa-t .... (**sat**)		r-uuuuu-g .... (**rug**)
		k-aaaaa-p .... (**cap**)

==

NEW SOUND: (Phonemic Awareness)
Lower Case:

a

@   *   >>

Capital Letter:

A

@   *   >>

Lower Case:

m

@   *   >>

Capital Letter:

M

@   *   >>

Lower Case:

n

@   *   >>

Capital Letter:

N

@   *   >>

SOUND PRACTICE:

INTRODUCTION: **Let's practice our sounds.**   (Point to the @ by the first sound).

Lower Case:

m   n

@   *   >>   @   *   >>

a   N

@   *   >>   @   *   >>

M   A

@   *   >>   @   *   >>

a   n

@   *   >>   @   *   >>

SOUNDING IT OUT: (Sound by Sound blending):
    Model: Teacher sounds out word, says the word.
    Lead: Teacher leads children in sounding out the word, saying it.
    Test: Students sound out the word, say it.

an
@   *   *   >>

am
@   *   *   >>

HIGH FREQUENCY WORDS – SIGHT WORD MEMORIZATION:

I
@   ^   >>

READING THE STORY:

I am ...
@ ^ @ *   *   ^Students say their name here^ >>

KINDERGARTEN TRANSITION DAY 2:

HEARING SOUNDS IN WORDS: (Phonemic Awareness)

**DO NOT STOP BETWEEN THE SOUNDS...

===

aaaaa-t .... (**at**)   fffff-aaaaa-nnnnn ....(**fan**)

sssss-aaaaa-t .... (**sat**)   mmmmm-aaaaa-p ....(**map**)

k-aaaaa-t .... (**cat**)   r-uuuuu-g ....(**rug**)

d-aaaaa-d .... (**dad**)   k-aaaaa-p ....(**cap**)

mmmmm-ooooo-p .... (**mop**)   mmmmm-aaaaa-nnnnn ....(**man**)

===

NEW SOUND: (Phonemic Awareness)
Lower Case:

S

@   *   >>

Capital Letter:

S

@   *   >>

NEW SOUND: (Phonemic Awareness)
Lower Case:

p

@   >   >>

Capital Letter:

P

@   >   >>

NEW SOUND: (Phonemic Awareness)
Lower Case:

c

@   >   >>

Capital Letter:

C

@   >   >>

SOUND REVIEW: (Phonemic Awareness)

a   m

@   *   >>   @   *   >>

s   c   p

@   *   >>   @   >   >>   @   >   >>

n   a

@   *   >>   @   *   >>

p   c   s

@   >   >>   @   >   >>   @   *   >>

SOUNDING OUT WORDS: (Sound by Sound blending):
    Model: Teacher sounds out word, says the word.
    Lead: Teacher leads children in sounding out the word, saying it.
    Test: Students sound out the word, say it.

an   am
@   *   *   >>   @   *   *   >>

man   can
@   *   *   *   >>   @   >   *   *   >>

pan   Nan
@   >   *   *   >>   @   *   *   *   >>

Pam   Sam
@   >   *   *   >>   @   *   *   *   >>

sap   map

@   *   *   >   >>   @   *   *   >   >>

man   pan

@   *   *   *   >>   @   >   *   *   >>

am   an

@   *   *   >>   @   *   *   >>

SIGHT WORD MEMORIZATION:

Tell: This word is ….
Spell: Spell it…"I"
Tell: What word is it? Students: "I".

I

@   ^   >>

a

@   ^   >>

(This word is "uh")

to

@   ^   ^   >>

like

@   ^   ^   ^   ^   >>

READING THE ARTICLE WITH A WORD:

The Sound: The word:

a   a

@   *   (aaaaa) >>   @   ^   (uh)   >>

READING IT AS A WORD:

a man

@   ^   >>   @   *   *   *   >>

READING THE STORY

I am Pam.
@   ^   @   *   *   @   >   *   *   >>

I am Nan.
@   ^   @   *   *   @   *   *   *   >>

I am Sam.
@   ^   @   *   *   @   *   *   *   >>

I am a man.
@   ^   @   *   *   @   ^   @   *   *   *   >>

I am Pam.
@   ^   @   *   *   @   >   *   *   >>

I am Nan.

@   ^   @   *   *   @   *   *   *   >>

I am Sam.

@   ^   @   *   *   @   *   *   *   >>

I am a man.

@   ^   @   *   *   @   ^   @   *   *   *   >>

I like Pam.

@   ^   @   ^   ^   ^   ^   @   >   *   *   >>

I like Nan.

@   ^   @   ^   ^   ^   ^   @   *   *   *   >>

I like Sam.

@ ^ @ ^ ^ ^ ^ @ * * * >>

I like Pam.

@ ^ @ ^ ^ ^ ^ @ > * * >>

I like Nan.

@ ^ @ ^ ^ ^ ^ @ * * * >>

I like Sam.

@ ^ @ ^ ^ ^ ^ @ * * * >>

KINDERGARTEN TRANSITION DAY 3:

HEARING SOUNDS IN WORDS: (Phonemic Awareness)

**DO NOT STOP BETWEEN THE SOUNDS...

==

aaaaa-nnnnn .... (**an**)   fffff-aaaaa-nnnnn ....(**fan**)

p-aaaaa-nnnnn .... (**pan**)   mmmmm-aaaaa-p ....(**map**)

sssss-aaaaa-d .... (**sad**)   rrrrr-uuuuu-g ....(**rug**)

sssss-aaaaa-t .... (**sat**)   g-aaaaa-sssss ....(**gas**)

mmmmm-iiiii-sssss .... (**miss**)   mmmmm-aaaaa-nnnnn ....(**man**)

==

NEW SOUNDS: (Phonemic Awareness)
Lower Case:

t

@   >   >>

Capital Letter:

T

@   >   >>

NEW SOUND: (Phonemic Awareness)
Lower Case:

f

@   *   >>

Capital Letter:

F

@   *   >>

Lower Case:

d

@   >   >>

Capital Letter:

D

@   >   >>

SOUND REVIEW: (Phonemic Awareness)

m   a

@   *   >>   @   *   >>

s   p   c

@   *   >>   @   >   >>   @   >   >>

f   a

@   *   >>   @   *   >>

d   t   n

@   >   >>   @   >   >>   @   *   >>

SOUNDING OUT WORDS: (Sound by Sound blending):

can

@   >   *   *   >>

Sam

@   *   *   *   >>

tan

@   >   *   *   >>

fan

@   *   *   *   >>

pan

@   >   *   *   >>

mad

@   *   *   >   >>

mat

@   *   *   >   >>

sat

@   *   *   >   >>

tap

@   >   *   >   >>

map

@   *   *   >   >>

sad

@   *   *   >   >>

fan

@   *   *   *   >>

pass

@   >   *   *   *   >>

man

@   *   *   *   >>

SIGHT WORD MEMORIZATION:

I

@   ^   >>

a

@   ^   >>

see

@   ^   ^   ^   >>

the

@   ^   ^   ^   >>

to   like
@   ^   ^   >>   @   ^   ^   ^   ^   >>

we
@   ^   ^   >>

go
@   ^   ^   >>

the   see
@   ^   ^   ^   >>   @   ^   ^   ^   >>

READING THE ARTICLE "a" WITH A WORD:

The Sound: The word:

a   a

@   *   (aaaaa) >>   @   ^   (uh)   >>

READING IT AS A WORD:

a man

@   ^   >>   @   *   *   *   >>

a map

@   ^   >>   @   *   *   *   >>

a sad man

@   ^   >> @   *   *   >   @   *   *   *   >>

READING THE STORY :

I like the fan.
@ ^ @ ^ ^ ^ ^ @ ^ ^ ^ @ * * * >>

I see the map.
@ ^ @ ^ ^ ^ @ ^ ^ ^ @ * * > >>

We can go to
@ ^ ^ @ > * * @ ^ ^ @ ^ ^ >>

see Pam. We
@ * * * @ ^ * * @ ^ ^ >>

can go to see a
@ > * * @ ^ ^ @ ^ ^ @ * * * @ ^

map .   We can
@   *   *   >   @   ^   ^   @   >   *   *   >>

see a sad man.
@   ^   ^   ^   @   ^   @   *   *   >   @   *   *   *   >>

We can go see
@   ^   ^   @   >   *   *   @   ^   ^   @   ^   ^   ^   >>

sad, sad Sam!
@   *   *   >   @   *   *   >   @   *   *   *

KINDERGARTEN TRANSITION DAY 4:

HEARING SOUNDS IN WORDS: (Phonemic Awareness)

**DO NOT STOP BETWEEN THE SOUNDS...

===

sssss-aaaaa-t .... **(sat)**	sssss-aaaaa-t .... **(sat)**
lllll-aaaaa-fffff .... **(laugh)**	mmmmm-iiiii-sssss .... **(miss)**
c-aaaaa-p .... **(cap)**	fffff-aaaaa-nnnnn .... **(fan)**
rrrrr-aaaaa-k .... **(rack)**	mmmmm-aaaaa-p .... **(map)**
p-aaaaa-n .... **(pan)**	rrrrr-uuuuu-g .... **(rug)**
sssss-aaaaa-d .... **(sad)**	g-aaaaa-sssss .... **(gas)**

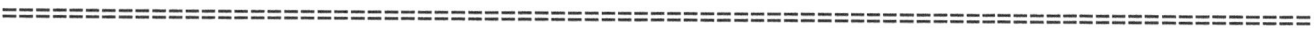

===

REVIEWING SOUNDS: (Phonemic Awareness)

a   m

@   *   >>   @   *   >>

n   d   p

@   *   >>   @   >   >>   @   >   >>

f   t

@   *   >>   @   >   >>

a   c   s

@   *   >>   @   >   >>   @   *   >>

SOUNDING CAPITAL LETTERS: (Phonemic awareness)

C   S

@   >   >>   @   *   >>

N   D   T

@   *   >>   @   >   >>   @   >   >>

A

P

@   *   >>   @   >   >>

T   M   F

@   >   >>   @   *   >>   @   *   >>

SOUND REVIEW: (Phonemic Awareness)

m   a

@   *   >>   @   *   >>

S   p   c

@   *   >>   @   >   >>   @   >   >>

f   a

@   *   >>   @   *   >>

d   t   n

@   >   >>   @   >   >>   @   *   >>

SOUNDING OUT WORDS: (Sound by Sound blending):

mat   Tam

@   *   *   >   >>   @   >   *   *   >>

fan   tan

@   *   *   *   >>   @   >   *   *   >>

man

@   *   *   *   >>

Sam

@   *   *   *   >>

pass

@   >   *   *   *   >>

tap

@   >   *   >   >>

sat

@   *   *   >   >>

and

@   *   *   >   >>

sad

@   *   *   >   >>

can

@   >   *   *   >>

Dan

@   >   *   *   >>

mad

@   *   *   >   >>

SIGHT WORD MEMORIZATION:

I

@   ^   >>

a

@   ^   >>

HIGH FREQUENCY WORDS:

    High frequency words are usually called sight words. At this time in the program the program also refers to words that the students cannot sound out, because the students have not been introduced to the sounds as yet. These words are necessary so that the students can read the anchored text story successfully and be able to work on higher level skills. Therefore it is important to get the students to commit the words to memory. Memorizing the word and not sounding it out makes the word a "sight word." There are three strategies for learning sight words. *First* is spelling and saying the words. The *second* is sounding them out wrong and saying them right. The third it finding a creative connection to the word. It often is between the shape or looks of the word. Sometimes it can be a limerick or poem. It also can be a similarity of a sound in the word that sparks the name of the word. If you choose the common spell the word, it is suggested: "Say the word," "spell the word," "say the word."

SIGHT WORD MEMORIZATION:

is

@   ^   ^   >>

are
@ ^ ^ ^ >>

We
@ ^ ^ >>

go
@ ^ ^ >>

the
@ ^ ^ ^ >>

like
@ ^ ^ ^ ^ >>

see
@ ^ ^ ^ >>

is
@ ^ ^ >>

are   I
@   ^   ^   ^   >>   @   ^   >>

a   to
@   ^   >>   @   ^   ^   >>

READING THE ARTICLE "a" WITH A WORD:

The Sound: The word:

a   a
@   *   (aaaaa)   >>   @   ^   (uh)   >>

READING IT AS A WORD:

a man
@   ^   >>   @   *   *   *   >>

a can
@   ^   >>   @   >   *   *   >>

a cat
@   ^   >> @   >   *   >   >>

READING THE STORY:

I am Cam the
@   ^   @   *   *   @   >   *   *   @   ^   ^   ^   >>

cat.
@   >   *   >

I see a can. I
@   ^   @ ^   ^   ^   @   ^   @   ^   *   *   @   ^

pass the can.
@   >   *   *   *   @   ^   ^   ^   @   >   *   *   >>

I see a man.
@   > @ ^   ^   ^   @   ^   @   *   *   *   >>

I pass the man.
@   > @   >   *   *   *   @ ^   ^   ^   @   *   *   *   >>

I am Cam,
@   ^ @   *   *   @   >   *   *   >>
>>

the fat cat!
@   ^   ^   ^   @   *   *   > @   >   *   >

KINDERGARTEN TRANSITION DAY 5:

HEARING SOUNDS IN WORDS: (Phonemic Awareness)

**DO NOT STOP BETWEEN THE SOUNDS...

==

k-aaaaa-p .... **(cap)**   fffff-lllll-aaaaa-p ....**(flap)**

t-aaaaa-p .... **(tap)**   g-aaaaa-p ....**(gap)**

lllll-aaaaa-p .... **(lap)**   sssss-aaaaa-p ....**(sap)**

mmmmm-aaaaa-p .... **(map)**   t-rrrrr-aaaaa-p ....**(trap)**

==

RHYMING WORDS: **(1). Let me say all the words together. Tell me, how are they alike? (2). Show me one finger if they have the same beginning sound. Show me two fingers if they have the same ending sounds. I'll say them one more time. (3). Get ready to show me...** (Signal.) **Show me.** If there is a showing of one finger go back and make similar comparisons of the words. **When the endings sound the same that is called rhyming. These are rhyming words. (4). Here's a poem...**

While I'm wearing my cap,

I get water from the tap;

The thirsty cat sits in my lap;

While I'm reading my map.

REVIEWING SOUNDS: (Phonemic Awareness)

n   f

@   *   >>   @   *   >>

a   t   c

@   *   >>   @   >   >>   @   >   >>

m   d

@   *   >>   @   >   >>

s   p   a

@   *   >>   @   >   >>   @   *   >>

SOUNDING CAPITAL LETTERS: (Phonemic awareness)

A   S

@   *   >>   @   *   >>

N   D   T

@   *   >>   @   >   >>   @   >   >>

F   C

@   *   >>   @   >   >>

N   P   M

@   *   >>   @   >   >>   @   *   >>

SOUNDING OUT WORDS: (Sound by Sound blending):

man   fan

@   *   *   *   >>   @   *   *   *   >>

mat   sap

@   *   *   >   >>   @   *   *   >   >>

Dan   tan

@   >   *   *   >>   @   >   *   *   >>

sat   map

@   *   *   >   >>   @   *   *   >   >>

pan   mad

@   >   *   *   >>   @   *   *   >   >>

pass   tap

@   >   *   *   *   >>   @   >   *   >   >>

sad   can

@   *   *   >   >>   @   >   *   *   >>

HIGH FREQUENCY WORDS:

like

@   ^   ^   ^   ^   >>

Continue with each high frequency word:

to

@   ^   ^   >>

I

@   ^   >>

go

@   ^   ^   >

a

@   ^   >>

are

@   ^   ^   ^   >>

the   we
@   ^   ^   ^   >>   @   ^   ^   >>

see   to
@   ^   ^   ^ >>   @   ^   ^   >>

like   is
@   ^ ^   ^   ^   >>   @   ^   ^   >>

READING THE STORY:

Pam and I see

@   ^   *   *   @   *   *   >   @ ^ @ ^   ^   ^   >>

a cat.

@   ^   @   >   *   >   >>

The cat is fat.

@ ^   ^   ^   @   >   *   > @ ^   ^   @   *   *   >   >>

We like the cat.

@   ^   ^   @ ^ ^   ^   ^   @   ^   ^   ^   @   >   *   >   >

The cat is sad.

@   ^   ^   ^   @   >   *   > @ ^   ^   @   *   *   >   >>

We go to fan

@   ^   ^   @   ^   ^   @   ^   ^   @   *   *   *   >>

the cat.

@   ^   ^   ^   @   >   *   >   >>

We fan the cat

@   ^   ^   @ *   *   *   @^   ^   ^   @   >   *   > >>

and we tap the

@   *   *   >   @   ^   ^   @ >   *   >   @   ^   ^   ^   >>

cat. The cat is

@   >   *   >   @ ^   ^   ^ @ >   *   > @ ^ ^   >>

mad. We are

@   *   *   >   @   ^   ^   @ ^   ^   ^ >>

sad.

*   *   >   >>

LESSON 1 DAY 1

HEARING SOUNDS IN WORDS: (Phonemic Awareness)

**DO NOT STOP BETWEEN THE SOUNDS...
===

aaaaa-mmmmm .... (**am**)

mmmmm-aaaaa-nnnnn .... (**man**)

b-aaaaa-t .... (**bat**)

sssss-aaaaa-t .... (**sat**)

d-aaaaa-d .... (**dad**)

mmmmm-ooooo-p .... (**mop**)

fffff-aaaaa-nnnnn .... (**fan**)

mmmmm-aaaaa-p .... (**map**)

rrrrr-uuuuu-g .... (**rug**)

k-aaaaa-p .... (**cap**)

zzzzz-iiiii-p .... (**zip**)

k-aaaaa-t .... (**cat**)

P-aaaaa-t .... (**Pat**)

===

SOUND PRACTICE: (Phonemic Awareness)

REVIEWING SOUNDS: (Phonemic Awareness)

s   n   d

@   *   >>   @   *   >>   @   >   >>

c   m

@   >   >>   @   *   >>

t   f

@   >   >>   @   *   >>

a   p

@   *   >>   @   >   >>

SOUNDING CAPITAL LETTERS: (Phonemic awareness)

C   S

@   >   >>   @   *   >>

N   D   T

@   *   >>   @   >   >>   @   >   >>

S   C

@   *   >>   @   >   >>

T   N   D

@   >   >>   @   *   >>   @   >   >>

SOUNDING OUT WORDS: (Sound by Sound blending):

an   man

@ *   *   >>   @   *   *   *   >>

can   and

@   >   *   *   >>   @   *   *   >   >>

Dan   fan

@   >   *   *   >>   @   *   *   *   >>

at   sat

@   *   >   >>   @   *   *   >   >>

SOUNDING OUT WORDS: (Sound by Sound blending):

mat

@   *   *   >   >>

dad   mad

@   >   *   >   >>   @   *   *   >   >>

am

@   *   *   >>

Pam   Nan

@   >   *   *   >>   @   *   *   *   >>

at   cat

@   *   >   >>   @   >   *   >   >>

cap

@   >   *   >   >>

tap　map

@　>　*　>　>>　　@　*　*　>　>>

nap

@　*　*　>　>>

Cam　Sam

@　>　*　*　>>　　@　*　*　*　>>

HIGH FREQUENCY WORDS:

SIGHT WORD MEMORIZATION:

be
@   ^   ^   >>

you
@   ^   ^   ^   >>

with
@   ^   ^   ^   ^   >>

help
@   ^   ^   ^   ^   >>

play

@   ^   ^   ^   ^   >>

pal

@   ^   ^   ^   >>

are

@   ^   ^   ^   >>

I

@   ^   >>

The sound: The word:

a   @   *   >>   a   @   ^   >>

READING IT AS A WORD:

a   cat

@   ^   >> @   >   *   >   >>

a   can

@   ^   >> @   >   *   *   >>

a   fan

@   ^   >> @   *   *   *   >>

a cap

@   ^   >>   @   >   *   >   >>

a mat

@   ^   >>   @   *   *   >   >>

a nap

@   ^   >>   @   *   *   >   >>

REVIEW: **Do you remember these words?**

you   the
@   ^   ^   ^   >>   @   ^   ^   ^   >>

play   are
@   ^   ^   ^   ^   >>   @   ^   ^   ^   >>

be   pal
@   ^   ^   >>   @   ^   ^   ^   >>

with   help
@   ^   ^   ^   ^   >>   @   ^   ^   ^   ^   >>

READING THE STORY:
(Struggling Readers sound out word by word)

I am Nan.
@ ^ @ * * @ * * * >>

I like the cat.
@ ^ @ ^ ^ ^ ^ @ ^ ^ ^ @ > * > >>

I see the cat.
@ ^ @ ^ ^ ^ @ ^ ^ ^ @ > * > >>

I can pat the
@ ^ @ > * * @ > * > @ ^ ^ ^ >

cat. I can
@ > * > @ ^ @ > * * >>

play with the
@ ^ ^ ^ ^ @ ^ ^ ^ ^ @ ^ ^ ^ >>

cat. I can see
@ > * > @ ^ @ > * * @ ^ ^ ^ >>

the cat play
@ ^ ^ ^ @ > * > @ ^ ^ ^ ^ >>

with a cap.
@ ^ ^ ^ ^ @ ^ @ > * > >>

I can help the
@ ^ @ > * * @ ^ ^ ^ ^ @ ^ ^ ^ >>

cat play with

@   >   *   >   @   ^   ^   ^   ^   @   ^   ^   ^   >>

the cap.

@   ^   ^   ^   @   >   *   >   >>

LESSON 1 DAY 2

**DO NOT STOP BETWEEN THE SOUNDS...

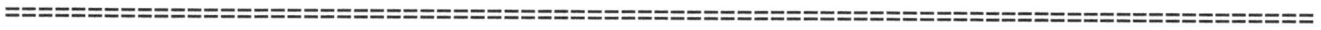

==

k-aaaaa-nnnnn .... (**can**)

sssss-aaaaa-t .... (**sat**)

mmmmm-aaaaa-d .... (**mad**)

t-aaaaa-nnnnn .... (**tan**)

D-aaaaa-nnnnn .... (**Dan**)

nnnnn-aaaaa-p .... (**nap**)

mmmmm-aaaaa-t .... (**mat**)

==

REVIEWING SOUNDS: (Phonemic Awareness)

f   t

@   *   >>   @   >   >>

a   c   s

@   *   >>   @   >   >>   @   *   >>

n
@   *   >>

p
@   >   >>

d
@   >   >>

m
@   *   >>

a
@   *   >>

REVIEWING SOUNDS: (Phonemic Awareness)

s
@   *   >>

c
@   >   >>

a
@   *   >>

t
@   >   >>

f
@   *   >>

SOUNDING CAPITAL LETTERS: (Phonemic awareness)

N   D   T

@   *   >>   @   >   >>   @   >   >>

S   C

@   *   >>   @   >   >>

T   N   D

@   >   >>   @   *   >>   @   >   >>

C   S

@   >   >>   @   *   >>

Dan   fan

@   >   *   *   >>   @   *   *   *   >>

can   and

@   >   *   *   >>   @   *   *   >   >>

an   man

@   *   *   >>   @   *   *   *   >>

dad   mad

@   >   *   >   >> @   *   *   >   >>

am

@   *   *   >>

at   sat

@   *   >   >>   @   *   *   >   >>

mat

@   *   *   >   >>

Pam   Nan

@   >   *   *   >>   @   *   *   *   >>

Nat

@   *   *   >   >>

cat

@   >   *   >   >>

cap

@   >   *   >   >>

nap

@   *   *   >   >>

Tad

@   >   *   >   >>

tan

@   >   *   *   >>

Cam

@   >   *   *   >>

Sam

@   *   *   *   >>

HIGH FREQUENCY WORDS:

SIGHT WORD MEMORIZATION:

the
@   ^   ^   ^   >>

be
@   ^   ^   >>

you
@   ^   ^   ^   >>

be
@   ^   ^   >>

pal
@   ^   ^   ^   >>

with
@   ^   ^   ^   ^   >>

help
@   ^   ^   ^   ^   >>

you
@   ^   ^   ^   >>

the
@   ^   ^   ^   >>

play
@   ^   ^   ^   ^   >>

SOUND OUT WRONG / SAY IT RIGHT:
Say the sound: (saying it wrong)   Say the word: (saying it right)

a   a

@   * (aaaaa)   >>   @   ^   (Uh)   >>

a   cat

@   ^   >> @   >   *   >   >>

a   cap

@   ^   @   >   *   >   >>

a   fan

@   ^   @   *   *   *   >>

a   can

@   ^   @   >   *   *   >>

a   map

@   ^   @   *   *   >   >>

a   nap

@   ^   @   *   *   >   >>

READING THE STORY

I like Nat and

@   ^   @ ^ ^   ^   ^   @   *   *   >   @   *   *   >   >>

Pam.

@   ^   *   *   >>

Nat and Pam

@   *   *   > @   *   *   >   @   >   *   *   >>

play with the

@   ^   ^   ^   ^   @   ^   ^ ^   ^   @   ^   ^   ^   >>

cat.

@   >   *   >   >>

Nat and Pam
@   *   *   >   @ *   *   >   @   >   *   *   >>

can nap.
@   >   *   *   @   *   *   >   >>

The cat can
@   ^   ^   ^   @   >   *   >   @   >   *   *   >>

nap.
@   *   *   >   >>

LESSON 1 DAY 3:　　HEARING SOUNDS IN WORDS (Phonemic Awareness):

Do not stop between the sounds.

===

b-aaaaa-t .... (**bat**)　　　　D-aaaaa-nnnnn .... (**Dan**)

fffff-aaaaa-t .... (**fat**)　　　　nnnnn-aaaaa-p .... (**nap**)

k-aaaaa-nnnnn .... (**can**)　　　　mmmmm-aaaaa-d .... (**mad**)

sssss-aaaaa-t .... (**sat**)　　　　t-aaaaa-nnnnn .... (**tan**)

mmmmm-aaaaa-d .... (**mad**)　　　　mmmmm-aaaaa-t .... (**mat**)

p-aaaaa-nnnnn .... (**pan**)　　　　rrrrr-aaaaa-t .... (**rat**)

fffff-iiiii-sh_sh_sh_sh_sh .... (**fish**)

===

REVIEWING SOUNDS: (Phonemic Awareness)

p　　　　t

@　　>　　>>　　　　@　　>　　>>

a　　　　c　　　　s

@　　*　　>>　　　　@　　>　　>>　　　　@　　*　　>>

71

n   f   d

@   *   >>   @   *   >>   @   >   >>

a   m

@   *   >>   @   *   >>

s   p   a

@   *   >>   @   >   >>   @   *   >>

t   f

@   >   >>   @   *   >>

n   f   d

@   *   >>   @   *   >>   @   >   >>

a   p

@   *   >>   @   >   >>

N   D   T

@   *   >>   @   >   >>   @   >   >>

F   P

@   *   >>   @   >   >>

C N T

@   >   >>   @   *   >>   @   >   >>

P S

@   >   >>   @   *   >>

SOUNDING OUT WORDS: (Sound by Sound blending):

cap

@   >   *   >

Pam

@   >   *   *   >>

tan

@   >   *   *

sat

@   *   *   >   >>

pan

@   >   *   *

mad

@   *   *   >   >>

tap

@   >   *   >

nap

@   *   *   >   >>

dad

@   >   *   >   >>

am

@   *   *   >>

pat

@   >   *   >   >>

sad

@   *   *   >   >>

fat

@   *   *   >   >>

dad

@   >   *   >   >>

Sam

@   *   *   *   >>

fan

@   *   *   *   >>

Nat   cat

@   *   *   >   @   >   *   >   >>

pad   can

@   >   *   >   @   >   *   *   >

Tad   pan

@   >   *   >   @   >   *   *   >>

man   nap

@   *   *   *   @   *   *   >   >>

Dan   Nan

@   >   *   *   @   *   *   *   >>

HIGH FREQUENCY WORDS:

SIGHT WORD MEMORIZATION:

the
@ ^ ^ ^ >>

you   I
@ ^ ^ ^ >>   @ ^ >>

be   a
@ ^ ^ >>   @ ^ >>

with   help
@ ^ ^ ^ ^ >>   @ ^ ^ ^ ^ >>

be

@   ^   ^

pal

@   ^   ^   ^   >>

play

@   ^   ^   ^   ^

I

@   ^   >>

you

@   ^   ^   ^

the

@   ^   ^   ^   >>

SOUND OUT WRONG / SAY IT RIGHT:
Say the sound: (saying it wrong)   Say the word: (saying it right)

a   a

@   * (aaaaa)   >>   @   ^ (Uh)   >>

a cat

@   ^   >> @   >   *   >   >>

a can

@   ^   >>   @   >   *   *   >>

a fan

@   ^   >>   @   *   *   *   >>

a   cap

@   ^   >>   @   >   *   >   >>

a   mat

@   ^   >>   @   *   *   >   >>

a   nap

@   ^   >>   @   *   *   >   >>

READING THE STORY:
(SOUNDING IT OUT/SPELLING WORD BY WORD with the STRUGGLING READERS)

Dan and Pat
@   >   *   *   @   *   *   >   @   >   *   >   >>

like me.
@ ^ ^ ^   ^   @ ^   ^   >>

I like Dan and
@ ^ @ ^ ^   ^   ^   @   >   *   *   @   *   *   >   >>

Pat.
@   >   *   >   >>

Dan and Pat
@   >   *   *   @   *   *   >   @   >   *   >   >>

play with me.
@   ^   ^   ^   ^   @   ^   ^   ^   ^   @   ^   ^   >>

We can tap the
@   ^   ^   @   >   *   *   @   >   *   >   @   ^   ^   ^   >>

pan.
@   >   *   *   >>

We can see
@   ^   *   ^   @   >   *   *   @   ^   ^   ^   >>

Dad nap.
@   >   *   >   @   *   *   >   >>

We can fan

@   ^   ^   @   >   *   *   @ *   *   *   >>

Dad.

@   >   *   >   >>

LESSON 1 DAY 4:

HEARING SOUNDS IN WORDS:

=====================================

fffff-aaaaa-t .... (**fat**)

k-aaaaa-nnnnn .... (**can**)

mmmmm-aaaaa-d .... (**mad**)

fffff-iiiii-sh_sh_sh_sh_sh .... (**fish**)

D-aaaaa-nnnnn .... (**Dan**)

nnnnn-aaaaa-p .... (**nap**)

t-aaaaa-nnnnn .... (**tan**)

mmmmm-aaaaa-t .... (**mat**)

rrrrr-aaaaa-t .... (**rat**)

fffff-aaaaa-d .... (**fad**)

mmmmm-aaaaa-nnnnn .... (**man**)

mmmmm-aaaaa-p .... (**map**)

p-aaaaa-lllll .... (**pal**)

sssss-aaaaa-t .... (**sat**)

rrrrr-aaaaa-p .... (**rap**)

fffff-aaaaa-nnnnn .... (**fan**)

=====================================

REVIEWING SOUNDS: (Phonemic Awareness)

f   t

@   *   >>   @   >   >>

a   c   s

@   *   >>   @   >   >>   @   *   >>

n   p   d

@   *   >>   @   >   >>   @   >   >>

m   a

@   *   >>   @   *   >>

REVIEWING SOUNDS: (Phonemic Awareness)

s   c   a

@   *   >>   @   >   >>   @   *   >>

t   f

@   >   >>   @   *   >>

n   f   d

@   *   >>   @   *   >>   @   >   >>

a   p

@   *   >>   @   >   >>

REVIEWING CAPITAL LETTER SOUNDS: (Phonemic awareness)

N　　　D　　　T

@　*　>>　@　>　>>　@　>　>>

S　　　C

@　*　>>　@　>　>>

F　　　A　　　M

@　*　>>　@　*　>>　@　*　>>

P　　　S

@　>　>>　@　*　>>

SOUNDING OUT WORDS: (Sound by Sound blending):

can   and

@   >   *   *   >>   @   *   *   >   >>

cap   tan

@   >   *   >   >>   @   >   *   *   >>

tap   cat

@   >   *   >   >>   @   >   *   >   >>

sat   dad

@   *   *   >   >>   @   >   *   >   >>

sad   fan

@   *   *   >   >>   @   *   *   *   >>

pat

@   >   *   >   >>

mad

@   *   *   >   >>

pan

@   >   *   *   >>

Pat

@   >   *   >   >>

fat

@   *   *   >   >>

nap

@   *   *   >   >>

map

@   *   *   >   >>

man

@   *   *   *   >>

pad

@   >   *   >   >>

Sam

@   *   *   *   >>

Pam

@   >   *   *   >>

Dan

@   >   *   *   >>

RECHECK HIGH FREQUENCY WORDS:

a

@ ^ >>

pal

@ ^ ^ ^ >>

help

@ ^ ^ ^ ^ >>

you

@ ^ ^ ^ >>

the

@ ^ ^ ^ >>

play

@ ^ ^ ^ ^ >>

with

@ ^ ^ ^ ^ >>

be

@ ^ ^ >>

I

@ ^ >>

pals

@ ^ ^ ^ ^ >>

SOUND OUT WRONG / SAY IT RIGHT:
Say the sound: (saying it wrong)　　　　　　　Say the word: (saying it right)

a　　　　a
@　　　* (aaaaa)　>>　　　　@　　　^　(Uh)　　　>>

a cat
@　　　^　　>> @　　>　　*　　　>　　　>>

a can
@　　　^　　>>　　@　　>　　*　　*　　　>>

a fan
@　　　^　　>>　　@　　>　　*　　*　　　>>

a　cap

@　　　^　　>>　@　　>　　*　　　>　　　>>

a　mat

@　　　^　　>>　@　　　*　　*　　　>　　　>>

a　nap

@　　　^　　>>　@　　　*　　*　　　>　　　>>

READING THE STORY:
 (SOUNDING IT OUT/SPELLING WORD BY WORD with the Struggling Readers)

Nat likes Pat.

@   *   *   > @ ^ ^ ^   ^   * @ > *   >   >>

Pat is Nat's pal.

@   >   *   > @ ^ ^ @ * * > * @ ^ ^ ^ >>

Pat likes Nat.

@ >   *   > @ ^ ^ ^   ^   ^ @ * * >   >

Nat is Pat's pal.

@ >   *   > @ ^ ^ @ > * > * @ ^ ^ ^ >>

Pat and Nat

@　>　*　>　@　*　*　>　@　*　*　>　　　>>

play with the

@　^　^　^　^　@　^　^　^　^　@　^　^　^　　>>

cat.

@　>　*　>　　　>>

Pat and Nat pat

@　>　*　>　@　*　*　>　@　*　*　>　@　>　*　>　>>

the cat.

@　^　^　^　@　>　*　>　　　>>

Pat and Nat are

@   >   *   >   @   *   *   >   @   *   *   >   @ ^ ^ ^ >>

Pals.

@   ^   ^   ^   ^   >>

LESSON 1 DAY 5:

REVIEW DAY:

==

k-aaaaa-nnnnn ....(**can**)

nnnnn-aaaaa-p ....(**nap**)

t-aaaaa-nnnnn ....(**tan**)

rrrrr-aaaaa-t ....(**rat**)

mmmmm-aaaaa-nnnnn ....(**man**)

sssss-aaaaa-t ....(**sat**)

mmmmm-aaaaa-d ....(**mad**)

rrrrr-aaaaa-p ....(**rap**)

fffff-aaaaa-nnnnn ....(**fan**)

==

REVIEWING SOUNDS: (Phonemic Awareness)

s   t

@   *   >>   @   >   >>

n   c   s

@   *   >>   @   >   >>   @   *   >>

a   p   d

@   *   >>   @   >   >>   @   >   >>

m   f

@   *   >>   @   *   >>

SOUNDING OUT WORDS: (Sound by Sound blending):

Dan   tap
@   >   *   *   >>   @   >   *   >   >>

Sam   cat
@   *   *   *   >>   @   >   *   >   >>

and   sad
@   *   *   >   >>   @   *   *   >   >>

man   nap
@   *   *   *   >>   @   *   *   >   >>

Pam   fat
@   >   *   *   >>   @   *   *   >   >>

RECHECK HIGH FREQUENCY WORDS:

I

@ ^ >>

a

@ ^ >>

the

@ ^ ^ ^ >>

play

@ ^ ^ ^ ^ >>

help

@ ^ ^ ^ ^ >>

you

@ ^ ^ ^ >>

with

@ ^ ^ ^ ^ >>

be

@ ^ ^ >>

pal

@ ^ ^ ^ >>

SOUND OUT WRONG / SAY IT RIGHT:
Say the sound: (saying it wrong)   Say the word: (saying it right)

a   a

@   * (aaaaa)   >>   @   ^ (Uh)   >>

a cat

@   ^   >> @   >   *   >   >>

a can

@   ^   >>   @   >   *   *   >>

a fan

@   ^   >>   @   *   *   *   >>

101

a   cap

@   ^   >>   @   >   *   >   >>

a   mat

@   ^   >>   @   *   *   >   >>

a   nap

@   ^   >>   @   *   *   >   >>

READING THE STORY:
 (SOUNDING IT OUT/SPELLING IT WITH THE STRUGGLING READERS)

I can play
@   ^   @   >   *   *   @   ^   ^   ^   ^   >>

with you.
@   ^   ^   ^   ^   @   ^   ^   ^   >>

You can play
@   ^   ^   ^   @   >   *   *   @   ^   ^   ^   ^   >>

with me.
@   ^   ^   ^   ^   @   ^   ^   >>

We can play

@ ^ ^ @ > * * @ ^ ^ ^ ^ >>

with the cat.

@ ^ ^ ^ ^ @ ^ ^ ^ @ > * > >>

You are a

@ ^ ^ ^ @ ^ ^ ^ @ ^ >>

Pal.

@ ^ ^ ^ >>

LESSON 2 DAY 1:

HEARING SOUNDS IN WORDS:

==

mmmmm-ooooo-p .... (**mop**)

g-oe_oe_oe_oe_oe* .... (**go**)

rrrrr-uuuuu-g .... (**rug**)

zzzzz-iiiii-p .... (**zip**)

j-arr_arr_arr_arr_arr** .... (**jar**)

b-aaaaa-t .... (**bat**)

p-iiiii-nnnnn .... (**pin**)

rrrrr-iiiii-mmmmm .... (**rim**)

h-iiiii-t .... (**hit**)

h-iiiii-zzzzz .... (**his**)

fffff-iiiii-nnnnn .... (**fin**)

h-aaaaa-zzzzz .... (**has**)

    *oe is Universal English symbol for the long "O" sound
    **arr is the Universal English symbol for the vowel sound "ar" as in "car."

==

NEW SOUND: (Phonemic Awareness)

i

@   *   >>

it

@   *   >   >>

It

@   *   >   >>

fit

@   *   *   >   >>

Tim

@　　>　　*　　*　　>>

sit

@　*　　*　　>　　>>

NEW SOUND: (Phonemic Awareness)

*NOTE: _Teachers often mispronounce this sound_. It is not the "er" sound in "teach**er**!" It is the "r" sound in "**r**un." It is very similar to the "U" (as in blue) sound but with more pursed lips.

r

@　　*　　>>

R

@　　*　　>>

rat

@　*　　*　　>　　>>

NEW SOUND: (Phonemic Awareness)

h

@   >   >>

H

@   >   >>

h a t

@   >   *   >   >>

NEW SOUND: (Phonemic Awareness)

z

@   *   >>

z i p

@   *   *   >   >>

SOUNDING THE WORD WRONG AND SAYING THE WORD RIGHT: (High Frequency Word)
   ** prompt indicates that the letter has a different sound. Here it is "zzzzz" for "sssss."

We see: # is   but we say: # iz   What word? # is_z

@   *   *   >>   @   *   *   @   *   **   >>

We see: **as**   but we say: **az**   What word?   **as**z

@   *   *   >>   @   *   *   >>   @   *   **   >>

We see: **his**   but we say: **hiz**   What word?   **his**z

@   >   *   *   >>   @   >   *   *   >>   @   >   *   **   >>

We see: **has**   We say: **haz**   What word?   **has**z

@   >   *   *   >>   @   >   *   *   >>   @   >   *   **   >>

What words?

isz   **as**z

@   *   **   >>   @   *   **   >>

hisz   **has**z

@   >   *   **   >>   @   >   *   **   >>

SOUNDING OUT WORDS (Sound by Sound Blending):

rip
@   *   *   >   >>

zip
@   *   *   >   >>

hip
@   >   *   >   >>

fan
@   *   *   *   >>

ran
@   *   *   *   >>

him
@   >   *   *   >>

rat
@   *   *   >   >>

if
@   *   *   >>

SOUNDING OUT WORDS (Sound by Sound blending):

Tim   tan
@ > * * >>   @ > * * >>

fit   sit
@ * * > >>   @ * * > >>

pin   tin
@ > * * >>   @ > * * >>

sip   hit
@ * * > >>   @ > * > >>

Ram   rip
@ * * * >>   @ * * > >>

REVIEW WORDS:

can   and

@   >   *   *   >>   @   *   *   >   >>

cap   tan

@   >   *   >   >>   @   >   *   *   >>

tap   cat

@   >   *   >   >>   @   >   *   >   >>

sat   dad

@   *   *   >   >>   @   >   *   >   >>

sad   fan

@   *   *   >   >>   @   *   *   *   >>

for

@   ^   ^   ^   >>

as~z~

@   *   **   >>

have

@   ^   ^   ^   ^   ^

too

@   ^   ^   ^   >>

look

@   ^   ^   ^   ^   >>

what

@   ^   ^   ^   ^   >>

his~z~

@   >   *   **

he

@   ^   ^   >>

Please note that this symbol "" denotes "sound it wrong, say it right" format. Remind students of this.

has$_z$ is$_z$

@   >   *   **   @   *   **   >>

I   pal

@   ^   >>   @   ^   ^   ^   >>

help   you

@   ^   ^   ^   ^   >>   @   ^   ^   ^   >>

the   play

@   ^   ^   ^   >>   @   ^   ^   ^   ^   >>

with   be

@   ^   ^   ^   ^   >>   @   ^   ^   >>

Please note that this symbol "" denotes "sound it wrong, say it right" format. Remind students of this.

READING THE STORY:

Tim can pat
@   >   *   *   @   >   *   *   @   >   *   > >>

the fat cat.
@   ^   ^   ^   @   *   *   >   @   >   *   >   >>

The cat can
@   ^   ^   ^   @   >   *   >   @   >   *   *   >>

nap.
@   *   *   >

LESSON 2 DAY 2

HEARING SOUNDS IN WORDS:

==

b-aaaaa-t .... (**bat**)

lllll-aaaaa-mmmmm .... (**lamb**)

y-eeeee-lllll .... (**yell**)

fffff-oo_oo_oo_oo_oo-t* .... (**foot**)

d-ooooo-g .... (**dog**)

g-oe_oe_oe_oe_oe** .... (**go**)

k-oe_oe_oe_oe_oe-t** .... (**coat**)

s-oe_oe_oe_oe_oe** .... (**so**)

rrrrr-uuuuu-g .... (**rug**)

zzzzz-iiiii-p .... (**zip**)

j-arr_arr_arr_arr_arr*** .... (**jar**)

p-iiiii-nnnnn .... (**pin**)

rrrrr-iiiii-mmmmm .... (**rim**)

h-iiiii-t .... (**hit**)

h-iiiii-zzzzz .... (**his**)

h-aaaaa-zzzzz .... (**has**)

*oo is the Universal English symbol for "oo" as in "foot."
**oe is the Universal English symbol for the long "o" sound as in "boat."
***arr is the Universal English symbol for the vowel sound "ar" as in "car."
==

NEW SOUND: (Phonemic Awareness)

b

@   >   >>

CAPITAL LETTER:

B

@   >   >>

bat   tab

@   >   *   >   >>   @   >   *   >   >>

bit   rib

@   >   *   >   @   *   *   >   >>

bag   big

@   >   *   >   @   >   *   >   >>

cab   scab

@   >   *   >   @   *   >   *   >   >>

REVIEWING SOUNDS: (Phonemic Awareness)

i   r

@   *   >>   @   *   >>

z   h   p

@   *   >>   @   >   >>   @   >   >>

f   t

@   *   >>   @   >   >>

a   c   s

@   *   >>   @   >   >>   @   *   >>

SOUNDING OUT WORDS: (Sound by Sound blending):

fan
@   *   *   *   >>

zip
@   *   *   >   >>

hit
@   >   *   >   >>

rip
@   *   *   >   >>

rap
@   *   *   >   >>

him
@   >   *   *   >>

if
@   *   *   >   >>

ran
@   *   *   *   >>

SOUNDING OUT WORDS (Sound by Sound blending):

Ram   tan
@   *   *   *   >>   @   >   *   *   >>

pin   sit
@   >   *   *   >>   @   *   *   >   >>

hip   tin
@   >   *   >   >>   @   >   *   *   >>

sip   fit
@   *   *   >   >>   @   *   *   >   >>

Tim   zip
@   >   *   *   >>   @   *   *   >   >>

pat   mad

@   >   *   >   >>   @   *   *   >   >>

pan   Pat

@   >   *   *   >>   @   >   *   >   >>

fat   nap

@   *   *   >   >>   @   *   *   >   >>

map   man

@   *   *   >   >>   @   *   *   *   >>

pad   Sam

@   >   *   >   >>   @   *   *   *   >>

HIGH FREQUENCY WORDS:

for   is$_z$

@   ^   ^   ^   >>   @   *   **   >>

what   too

@   ^   ^   ^   ^   >> @   ^   ^   ^   >>

look   have

@   ^   ^   ^   ^   >>   @   ^   ^   ^   ^   >>

has$_z$ he

@   >   *   **   >>   @   ^   ^   >>

be

@   ^   ^   >>

the

@   ^   ^   ^   >>

with

@   ^   ^   ^   ^   >>

you

@   ^   ^   ^   >>

pal

@   ^   ^   ^   >>

play

@   ^   ^   ^   ^   >>

help

@   ^   ^   ^   ^   >>

I

@   ^   >>

READING THE STORY:

Pat can sit.
@   >   *   >   @   >   *   *   @   *   *   >

Pat has$_z$ a fan
@   >   *   >   @   >   *   **   @   ^   @   *   *   *

and a rat.
@   *   *   >   @   ^   @   *   *   >   >>

LESSON 2 DAY 3

HEARING SOUNDS IN WORDS

===

k-oe_oe_oe_oe_oe-lllll-d .... (cold)	k- oe_oe_oe_oe_oe-t* .... (coat)
nnnnn-eeeee-sssss-t .... (nest)	sssss-oe_oe_oe_oe_oe .... (so)
p-iiiii-g .... (pig)	rrrrr-uuuuu-g .... (rug)
mmmmm-eeeee-sssss .... (mess)	zzzzz-iiiii-p .... (zip)
b-lllll-ooooo-k .... (block)	p-iiiii-nnnnn .... (pin)
b-aaaaa-t .... (bat)	rrrrr-iiiii-mmmmm .... (rim)
lllll-aaaaa-mmmmm .... (lamb)	h-iiiii-t .... (hit)
yyyyy-eeeee-lllll .... (yell)	h-iiiii-zzzzz .... (his)
d-ooooo-g .... (dog)	fffff-iiiii-nnnnn .... (fin)
g-oe_oe_oe_oe_oe* .... (go)	h-aaaaa-zzzzz .... (has)

*oe is the Universal English symbol for the long "O" sound)
===

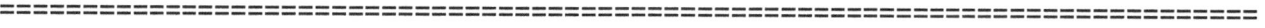

127

NEW SOUND: (Phonemic Awareness)

g

@   >   >>

CAPITAL LETTER:

G

@   >   >>

SOUNDING OUT WORDS:

bag   big

@   >   *   >   >>   @   >   *   >   >>

128

SOUNDING OUT WORDS:

rib
@   *   *   >   >>

bit
@   >   *   >   >>

gas
@   >   *   *   >>

gap
@   >   *   >   >>

bin
@   >   *   *   >>

fin
@   *   *   *   >>

fig
@   *   *   >   >>

zip
@   *   *   >   >>

tip
@   >   *   >   >>

Sid
@   *   *   >   >>

HIGH FREQUENCY WORDS:
SIGHT WORD MEMORIZATION:

for
@ ^ ^ ^ >>

what
@ ^ ^ ^ ^ >>

he
@ ^ ^ >>

too
@ ^ ^ ^ >>

look*
@ ^ ^ ^ ^ >>

see*
@ ^ ^ ^ >>

*Draw eyes in oo"s & ee's!

his$_z$
@ > * ** >>

have
@ ^ ^ ^ ^ >>

has$_z$
@ > * ** >>

is$_z$
@ * ** >>

REVIEW: Do you remember these words?

pal   a

@   ^ ^ ^ >>   @   ^   >>

the   I

@   ^ ^ ^ >>   @   ^   >>

with   play

@   ^ ^ ^ ^ >>   @   ^ ^ ^ ^   >>

help   be

@   ^ ^ ^ ^ >>   @   ^   ^   >>

you

@   ^ ^ ^ >>

READING THE STORY:
(Sounding it out/spelling it word by word with struggling readers)

Sam had a
@ > * *   @ > * > @ ^ >>

cat. Tig had
@ > * >   @ > * > @ > * > >>

a pig. Pam
@ ^ @ > * >   @ > * * >>

and Nan had
@ * * > @ * * * @ > * >
>>

a pig too!
@ ^ @ > * > @ ^ ^ ^ >>

LESSON 2 DAY 4

HEARING SOUNDS IN WORDS

==

f-ee_ee_ee_ee_ee-t* .... (feet)

sssss-uuuuu-nnnnn .... (sun)

k-ae_ae_ae_ae_ae-p .... (cape)

sssss-nnnnn-aaaaa-p .... (snap)

rrrrr-ae_ae_ae_ae_ae-nnnnn .... (rain)

k-oe_oe_oe_oe_oe-lllll-d .... (cold)

nnnnn-eeeee-sssss-t .... (nest)

p-iiiii-g .... (pig)

mmmmm-eeeee-sssss .... (mess)

b-lllll-ooooo-k .... (block)

b-aaaaa-t .... (bat)

yyyyy-eeeee-lllll .... (yell)

d-ooooo-g .... (dog)

rrrrr-uuuuu-g .... (rug)

zzzzz-iiiii-p .... (zip)

*oe is the Universal English symbol for the long "o" sound)

REVIEWING SOUNDS: (Phonemic Awareness)

g   b

@   >   >>   @   >   >>

z   h   a

@   *   >>   @   >   >>   @   *   >>

r   i

@   *   >>   @   *   >>

h   g   z

@   >   >>   @   >   >>   @   *   >>

SOUNDING OUT WORDS: (Sound by Sound blending):

gap   big

@   >   *   >   >>   @   >   *   >   >>

rib   bin

@   *   *   >   >>   @   >   *   *   >>

gas   bag

@   >   *   *   >>   @   >   *   >   >>

bit   fin

@   >   *   >   >>   @   *   *   *   >>

fig   bam

@   *   *   >   >>   @   >   *   *   >>

HIGH FREQUENCY WORDS:
SIGHT WORD MEMORIZATION:

see

@　^　^　^　>>

what

@　^　^　^　^　>>

he

@　^　^　>>

too

@　^　^　^　>>

look

@　^　^　^　^　>>

his$_z$

@　*　*　**　>>

for

@　^　^　^　>>

have

@　^　^　^　^　>>

has$_z$

@　>　*　**　>>

is$_z$

@　*　**　>>

pal   a

@   ^   ^   ^   >>   @   ^   >>

the   I

@   ^   ^   ^   >>   @   ^   >>

help   you

@   ^   ^   ^   ^   >>   @   ^   ^   ^   >>

play   be

@   ^   ^   ^   ^   >>   @   ^   ^   >>

with

@   ^   ^   ^   ^   >>

READING THE STORY: Sounding it out word by word

Dan has$_z$ a
@   >   *   *   @   >   *   **   @   ^   >>

bat. He can
@   >   *   >   @   ^   ^   @   >   *   *

hit a big bag.
@   >   *   >   @   ^   @   >   *   >   @   >   *   >

His$_z$ pig bit
@   >   *   **   @   >   *   >   @   *   *   >

the bag.
@   ^   ^   ^   @   >   *   >

LESSON 2 DAY 5

HEARING SOUNDS IN WORDS

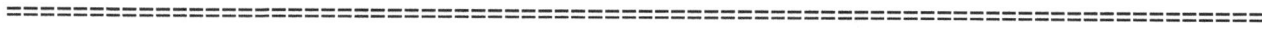

==

d-iiiii-g .... (dig)

nnnnn-oe_oe_oe_oe_oe-zzzzz .... (nose)*

p-ee_ee_ee_ee_ee-ch .... (peach)**

b-ae_ae_ae_ae_ae-k .... (bake)***

l-ooooo-g .... (log)

k-uuuuu-p .... (cup)

sssss-aaaaa-t .... (sat)

h-aaaaa-t .... (hat)

lllllll-ooooo-sssss-t .... (lost)

f-ee_ee_ee_ee_ee-t .... (feet)**

sssss-uuuuu-nnnnn .... (sun)

sssss-nnnnn-aaaaa-p .... (snap)

rrrrr-ae_ae_ae_ae_ae-nnnnn .... (rain)**

k-oe_oe_oe_oe_oe-lllll-d .... (cold)*

nnnnn-eeeee-sssss-t .... (nest)

p-iiiii-g .... (pig)

mmmmm-eeeee-sssss .... (mess)

b-lllll-ooooo-k .... (block)

*oe is Universal English symbol for the long "e" sound
**ee is Universal English symbol for the long "e" sound
***ae is Universal English symbol for the long "a" sound

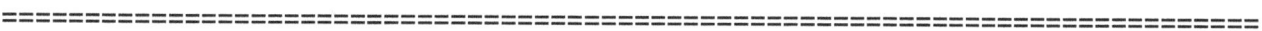

==

REVIEWING SOUNDS: (Phonemic Awareness)

r   g

@   *   >>   @   >   >>

z   h   a

@   *   >>   @   >   >>   @   *   >>

i   b

@   *   >>   @   >   >>

z   h   g

@   *   >>   @   >   >>   @   >   >>

SOUNDING OUT WORDS:

rib
@   *   *   >   >>

bin
@   >   *   *   >>

gap
@   >   *   >   >>

big
@   >   *   >   >>

bit
@   >   *   >   >>

fin
@   *   *   *   >>

gas
@   >   *   *   >>

bag
@   >   *   >   >>

fig
@   *   *   >   >>

zip
@   *   *   >   >>

SIGHT WORD MEMORIZATION:

has$_z$

@   >   *   **   >>

is$_z$

@   *   **   >>

see

@   ^   ^   ^   >>

what

@   ^   ^   ^   ^   >>

look

@   ^   ^   ^   ^   >>

his$_z$

@   >   *   **   >>

he

@   ^   ^   >>

too

@   ^   ^   ^   >>

for

@   ^   ^   ^   >>

have

@   ^   ^   ^   ^   >>

REVIEW: Do you remember these words?

play   be
@   ^   ^   ^   ^   >>   @   ^   ^   >>

the   I
@   ^   ^   ^   >>   @   ^   >>

help   you
@   ^   ^   ^   ^   >>   @   ^   ^   ^   >>

a   pal
@   ^   >>   @   ^   ^   ^   >>

with
@   ^   ^   ^   ^   >>

READING THE STORY: Sounding it out word by word

Tim can pat
@ > * * @ > * * @ > * > >>

the fat cat.The
@ ^ ^ ^ @ * * > @ > * > @ ^ ^ ^

cat can nap.
@ > * > @ > * * @ * * >

Pat can sit.
@ > * > @ > * * @ * * >

Pat has_z a fan

@ > * > @ > * ** @ ^ @ * * *

and a rat.

@ * * > @ ^ @ * * > >>

Sam had a

@ * * * @ > * > @ ^ >>

cat. Tig had

@ > * > @ > * > @ > * >

a pig. Sam

@ ^ @ > * > @ * * *

and Nan had

@ * * > @ * * * @ > * >

a pig too!

@   >   @   >   *   >   @   ^   ^   ^   >>

Dan has_z a

@   >   *   *   @   >   *   **   @   ^   >>

bat. He can

@   >   *   >   @   ^   ^   @   >   *   *   >>

hit a big bag.

@   >   *   >   @   ^   @   >   *   >   @   >   *   >

His_z pig bit

@   >   *   **   @   >   *   >   @   *   *   >

the bag.

@   ^   ^   ^   @   >   *   >

APPENDIX

Take-It-Home Worksheets

Handprinting Worksheets

Name:

Date:

KTDay 1

Parents: Your child is successful in reading in the classroom if he or she can read this without mistakes. Take time to read the Take-It-Home with your child every day. If you do, you are helping your child learn to read. ***The Italicized words are words that your child needs to memorize.*** The other words your child can "sound out."

I am

Name:

Date: _____ KTDay1

I am

I am

I am

I am

I

>

Name: _____

Date: _____

KTDay 2

Parents: Your child is successful in reading in the classroom if he or she can read this without mistakes. Take time to read the Take-It-Home with your child every day. If you do, you are helping your child learn to read. ***The Italicized words are words that your child needs to memorize.*** The other words your child can "sound out."

I am Pam.   *I* am Nan.

I like Pam.   *I like* Nan.

I like Sam.

Name:

Date:

I am Pam.

I am

I

I am Sam.

I am

I

Name: _____

Date: _____

KTDay 3

Parents: Your child is successful in reading in the classroom if he or she can read this without mistakes. Take time to read the Take-It-Home with your child every day. If you do, you are helping your child learn to read. ***The Italicized words are words that your child needs to memorize.*** The other words your child can "sound out."

I like the fan.

I see the map.

We can *see a* man.

We can *see a* sad man.

Name:

Date: KTDay3

I see the man.

I see

I

We see the man.

We see

>

Name: _____

Date: _____

KTDay 4

Parents: Your child is successful in reading in the classroom if he or she can read this without mistakes. Take time to read the Take-It-Home with your child every day. If you do, you are helping your child learn to read. ***The Italicized words are words that your child needs to memorize.*** The other words your child can "sound out."

I am Cam *the* cat. *I see a* can.
I pass *the* can. *I see a* man.
I pass *the* man. *I* am Cam *the* fat cat!

Name:

Date: KTDay4

I see the cat.

I see

>

I see the man.

I see

Date:

Parents: Your child is successful in reading in the classroom if he or she can read this without mistakes. Take time to read the Take-It-Home with your child every day. If you do, you are helping your child learn to read. ***The Italicized words are words that your child needs to memorize.*** The other words your child can "sound out."

I am Sam.   *I* am *a* man.
Pam and *I see a* cat.
The cat *is* fat.   *We like the* cat.
We go to fan *the* cat.
We tap *the* cat.
The cat *is* mad.   *I am* sad.

Name:

Date:

I am sad Sam.

I

>

The cat is mad.

>

>

Name: _____

Date: _____

Parents: Your child is successful in reading in the classroom if he or she can read this without mistakes. Take time to read the Take-It-Home with your child every day. If you do, you are helping your child learn to read. ***The Italicized words are words that your child needs to memorize.*** The other words your child can "sound out."

The cat and Nan sat.

Name: Date: L1D1

The cat and Nan sat.

Name: _____

Date: _____

L1Day 2

Parents: Your child is successful in reading in the classroom if he or she can read this without mistakes. Take time to read the Take-It-Home with your child every day. If you do, you are helping your child learn to read. ***The Italicized words are words that your child needs to memorize.*** The other words your child can "sound out."

Nat and *the* cat sat.

Name: Date: L1D2

Nat and the cat sat.

Name: _____

Date: _____

L1Day 3

Parents: Your child is successful in reading in the classroom if he or she can read this without mistakes. Take time to read the Take-It-Home with your child every day. If you do, you are helping your child learn to read. ***The Italicized words are words that your child needs to memorize.*** The other words your child can "sound out."

Pam and *the* cat can nap.

Name: Date: L1D3

Pam and the cat nap.

Name:

Date:

Parents: Your child is successful in reading in the classroom if he or she can read this without mistakes. Take time to read the Take-It-Home with your child every day. If you do, you are helping your child learn to read. ***The Italicized words are words that your child needs to memorize.*** The other words your child can "sound out."

Pat and *the* cat can *play*.

Name: Date: L1D4

Pat and the cat play.

Name:
_____

Date:
_____   L1Day 5

Parents: Your child is successful in reading in the classroom if he or she can read this without mistakes. Take time to read the Take-It-Home with your child every day. If you do, you are helping your child learn to read. ***The Italicized words are words that your child needs to memorize.*** The other words your child can "sound out."

Nat and *the* cat sat.
Pam and *the* cat can
nap. Pat and *the* cat
can *play*.

Name: Date: L1D5

Nat and the cat sat.

Pat and the cat play.

Name:

Date:

L2Day 1

Parents: Your child is successful in reading in the classroom if he or she can read this without mistakes. Take time to read the Take-It-Home with your child every day. If you do, you are helping your child learn to read. ***The Italicized words are words that your child needs to memorize.*** The other words your child can "sound out."

Tim can pat *the* fat cat.
The cat can nap.

Name: Date: L2D1

Tim can pat the cat

The cat can nap.

Name: _____

Date: _____

Parents: Your child is successful in reading in the classroom if he or she can read this without mistakes. Take time to read the Take-It-Home with your child every day. If you do, you are helping your child learn to read. ***The Italicized words are words that your child needs to memorize.*** The other words your child can "sound out."

Pat can sit. Pat *has*z *a* fan and *a* rat.

Name: Date: L2D2

Pat can sit and nap.

Pat has a fan and rat.

Name: _____

Date: _____

L2Day 3

Parents: Your child is successful in reading in the classroom if he or she can read this without mistakes. Take time to read the Take-It-Home with your child every day. If you do, you are helping your child learn to read. ***The Italicized words are words that your child needs to memorize.*** The other words your child can "sound out."

Sam *had a* cat.
Tig *had a* pig. Pam
and Nan *had a* pig *too*!

Name: Date: L2D3

Sam had a cat and pig.

Nan had a pig too!

Name: _____

Date: _____

L2Day 4

Dan *has*z *a* bat.
He can hit *a* big bag.
*His*z pig bit *the* bag.

Name: Date: L2D4

Dan has a bat and bag.

His pig bit the bag.

Name: _____

Date: _____

L2Day 5

Parents: Your child is successful in reading in the classroom if he or she can read this without mistakes. Take time to read the Take-It-Home with your child every day. If you do, you are helping your child learn to read. ***The Italicized words are words that your child needs to memorize.*** The other words your child can "sound out."

Tim can pat *the* fat cat. *The* cat can nap. Pat can sit. Pat *has*$_z$ *a* fan and *a* rat. Sam *had a* cat. Tig *had a* pig. Sam and Nan *had a* pig too! Dan *has*$_z$ *a* bat. He can hit *a* big bag. *His*$_z$ pig bit *the* bag.

Name: Date: L1D5

Pat has a fan and cat.

Tig had a pig and a rat.

www.ingramcontent.com/pod-product-compliance
Lightning Source LLC
Chambersburg PA
CBHW081630040426
42449CB00014B/3249